THE SCIENCE BEHIND
NATURAL
DISASTERS

VOLCANOES

THE SCIENCE BEHIND FIERY ERUPTIONS

Dr. Alvin Silverstein, Virginia Silverstein,
and Laura Silverstein Nunn

Enslow Publishers, Inc.
40 Industrial Road
Box 398
Berkeley Heights, NJ 07922
USA
http://www.enslow.com

Library of Congress Cataloging-in-Publication Data:

Silverstein, Alvin.
   Volcanoes : the science behind fiery eruptions / Alvin Silverstein, Virginia
Silverstein, and Laura Silverstein Nunn.
      p. cm. — (The science behind natural disasters)
   Includes bibliographical references and index.
   Summary: "Examines the science behind volcanoes, including what causes
them to erupt, the inner-workings of a volcano, underwater volcanoes, and
how to stay safe during an eruption"—Provided by publisher.
   ISBN-13: 978-0-7660-2972-9
   ISBN-10: 0-7660-2972-7
   1. Volcanoes—Juvenile literature. I. Silverstein, Virginia B. II. Nunn, Laura
Silverstein. III. Title.
   QE521.3.S53785 2010
   551.21–dc22

                       2008042866

Printed in the United States of America

10 9 8 7 6 5 4 3 2 1

To Our Readers:
We have done our best to make sure all Internet Addresses in this book were
active and appropriate when we went to press. However, the author and the
publisher have no control over and assume no liability for the material avail-
able on those Internet sites or on other Web sites they may link to. Any com-
ments or suggestions can be sent by e-mail to comments@enslow.com or to
the address on the back cover.

♻ Enslow Publishers, Inc., is committed to printing our books on recycled
paper. The paper in every book contains 10% to 30% post-consumer waste
(PCW). The cover board on the outside of each book contains 100% PCW.
Our goal is to do our part to help young people and the environment too!

Illustration Credits: © Andrea Danti, Shutterstock®, p. 13; Associated Press,
pp. 17, 22, 34; © Bruce Davidson / naturepl.com, p. 1, 8; © Doug Perrine /
Seapics.com, p. 26; Enslow Publishers, Inc., p. 11; Ewing Krainin / Photo
Researchers, Inc., p. 24;© iofoto, Shutterstock®, p. 31; J. D. Griggs / U.S.
Geological Survey, p. 20; Krafft / Explorer / Photo Researchers, Inc., p. 37;
NASA Jet Propulsion Laboratory (NASA–JPL), p. 24; National
Oceanographic and Atmospheric Administration (NOAA), p. 28; OAR /
National Undersea Research Program (NURP) / NOAA, pp. 32, 33; P.
Bourseiller—J. Durieux / Photo Researchers, Inc., p. 42; Stephen & Donna
O'Meara / Photo Researchers, Inc., p. 19; U.S. Geological Survey, pp. 4, 6, 25,
40, 41; Viktor Pryymachuk / Shutterstock®, p. 36; Xinhua / Landov, p. 16.

Cover Illustration: © Bruce Davidson / naturepl.com.

CONTENTS

Mount St. Helens in Washington State

was once famous for its nearly perfect cone shape. This snowcapped mountain was surrounded by thick forests and beautiful rivers and streams. But all that changed on May 18, 1980, when the top of the mountain exploded.

Mount St. Helens is a volcano. In 1980, it had been quiet for 123 years. But there were some warning signs that it was waking up. In the middle of March of that year, small earthquakes shook the mountain. On March 27, steam blasted through the snow and ice at the peak. The explosion created a large crater, or hole, that was 396 meters (1,300 feet) wide. That was only the beginning.

On Sunday morning, May 18, 1980, a magnitude 5.1 earthquake shook Mount St. Helens. The massive volcanic eruption sent volcanic ash, steam, water, and debris to a height of 60,000 feet.

By May 17, 1980, there had been more than ten thousand earthquakes. A big bulge, 137 meters (450 feet) wide, formed on the side of the mountain.[1] The next morning, May 18, right after a strong earthquake, the bulge burst. Rocks, ash, gases, and steam blasted up and out at 483 kilometers (300 miles) per hour. Then this volcano mixture fell down to cover the surrounding area.[2] The hot rocks and gases melted part of the ice cap. Water mixed with the rocks to form mud. Huge mudflows poured down the mountainside, knocking down trees and destroying bridges and homes.

Geologist Norman Banks walks over fallen timber near the headwaters of the Green River in Skamania County, Washington, just a few weeks after the 1980 eruption of Mount St. Helens. The eruption damaged more than 250 square miles of land.

An hour later, the volcano exploded again. This time, super-hot, liquid rock called lava gushed out of the crater. During the hours that followed, Mount St. Helens continued to erupt, pouring out bursts of steam, ash, gases, and hot rocks. By the end of the day, winds had blown more than 500 million tons of ash eastward.[3] In Spokane, Washington, 402 kilometers (250 miles) away, the ash cloud blocked the afternoon sunlight. It was as dark as night.

The May 18 eruption caused a lot of damage. It killed fifty-seven people and huge numbers of wildlife. About 7,000 big game animals, including deer and elk, and 12 million baby salmon in fish hatcheries died.[4] The eruption knocked down as many trees as it would take to build about 300,000 houses.[5]

The story of Mount St. Helens as an active volcano did not end in May 1980. There were five other eruptions that summer and fall. More than a dozen eruptions, lava flows, and mudslides occurred until late 1986. Then the mountain quieted down, only to wake up again in 2004. Small eruptions continued through January 2008.[6] Scientists are still watching Mount St. Helens. They say it is one of the most dangerous volcanoes in the United States today.

UNDERSTANDING VOLCANOES

What exactly are volcanoes?

Like Mount St. Helens, most volcanoes are cone-shaped mountains. Are all mountains volcanoes? No, only volcanoes can erupt. The word "erupt" comes from a Latin word meaning "to break out." That's exactly what happens when a volcano erupts: The mountain breaks open, and some of its hot contents escape. Burning hot gases, steam, and rocks may burst into the air and slide down the side of the mountain.

Lava explodes into the air during an eruption in the Kimanura Volcano in the Democratic Republic of the Congo (formerly Zaire).

Where Did Volcanoes Get That Name?

The word *volcano* comes from Vulcan, the Roman god of fire. When an island near Sicily began to spit out puffs of smoke and fiery lava, the ancient Romans thought it was Vulcan's workshop. They believed that Vulcan was making weapons for the other gods. The thick gray cloud of ash was smoke from his furnace. The glowing rocks were sparks. The Romans called the island Vulcano. The word volcano, used to describe any mountain that can erupt, comes from this name.

What Is an Active Volcano?

Some volcanoes are very active. They continually rumble and puff out smoke, steam, and ash. Others have been quiet for centuries. However, volcanologists (scientists who study volcanoes) have found evidence in rocks that these volcanoes did erupt long ago. These scientists say a volcano is active if it is erupting or showing other signs of activity. These other signs include earthquakes, puffs of smoke, or leaking gases. A volcano that has been quiet for at least a few thousand years is said to be dormant. However, it could become active some time in the future. Some volcanoes are believed to be extinct. They have not shown any signs of activity for many thousands of years. Volcanologists do not think these volcanoes will ever erupt again.

Most of Earth's volcanoes are found in the Ring of Fire.

Inside Earth

Scientists believe there are about fifteen hundred active volcanoes on land. Fifty or sixty of them erupt each year.[1] Volcanoes are clustered along the edges of the Pacific Ocean. This group of volcanoes is

> **❋ It's a Fact! ❋**
> There are active volcanoes on every continent except Australia. They can even be found on frigid Antarctica!

known as the Ring of Fire. Why are there so many volcanoes in these places? The answer lies deep below Earth's surface.

Earth is made up of layers. The outer layer is the crust. It is solid rock. The crust is thickest under the continents and much thinner under the oceans.

The middle layer is the mantle. It makes up most of Earth. The mantle is also very hot. Temperatures range from 500 degrees Celsius (932 degrees Fahrenheit) to more than 4,000 degrees Celsius (7,200 degrees Fahrenheit). This is hot enough to melt rocks. Melted rocks form a liquid called magma.

The deepest layer is the core, at the center of Earth. It is extremely hot there—more than 6,000 degrees Celsius (10,000 degrees Fahrenheit)!

Moving Parts

Earth's rocky crust, together with a layer of hard mantle just beneath it, consists of about a dozen pieces. These pieces are called tectonic plates. The plates fit together like the pieces of a jigsaw puzzle. They float on a hot layer of mantle. The floating plates move about, sometimes pulling apart, crashing into each other, or rubbing sideways along their edges. This is a very slow process. The different plates move from 1 to 10 centimeters (less than half an inch to 4 inches) per year. But they are so huge that even these small, creeping movements can cause huge effects.

This cutaway diagram shows what is happening inside an active volcano.

Most volcanoes form at the edges of the tectonic plates. The movements of the plates create stresses, which can build up and cause cracks in the rocks. These stresses may be relieved by volcanic eruptions. Some volcanoes are found in the middle of the plates. They form in places called hot spots, where magma has seeped up through weak spots in the crust. Sometimes a chain of volcanoes may form at a hot spot. The Hawaiian Islands are a well-known example of a volcanic chain.

How Volcanoes Form

A volcano starts out in the upper part of Earth's mantle, where the rocks have melted into magma. Hot magma may ooze upward through gaps or cracks in the solid crust. Magma tends to rise because it contains some gases and is lighter than solid rock. As it melts the surrounding rock, the magma may form a magma chamber. This is a giant pool of magma under the surface. The magma in the chamber is under high pressure from the heavy weight of the crust above it. (Pressure is a pushing force.) Finally, the magma breaks through the surface and bursts out in an eruption.

When magma reaches the air, it becomes lava. The openings through which gases, lava, and other volcanic matter escape are called vents. In many volcanoes, the vent ends in a bowl-shaped crater at the top of the mountain. Some volcanoes also have vents on the side of the mountain.

Volcanoes may stay quiet for hundreds or even thousands of years and then suddenly erupt. But what makes a volcano erupt, and what happens during an eruption?

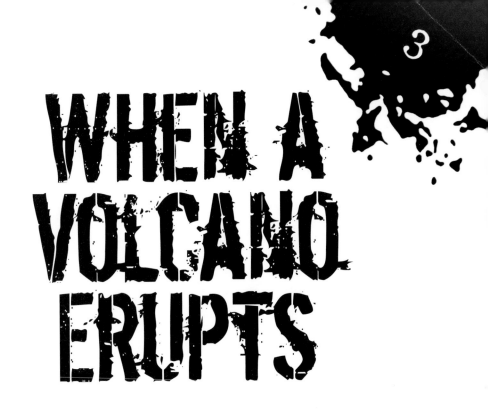

WHEN A VOLCANO ERUPTS

Have you ever shaken a can or bottle of soda before opening it? Like the magma under Earth's surface, soda is a mixture of liquid and gas under pressure. When you open the soda container, the pressure on the gas (carbon dioxide) drops suddenly. The gas expands rapidly, and bubbly soda explodes out, all over everything. That is a lot like what happens when a volcano erupts. While it is still trapped under rock, the hot magma is also under great pressure. When it reaches the surface, that pressure is suddenly removed. That is why a huge cloud of gas, ash, and rocks may shoot up into the air when a volcano erupts.

A huge cloud of ash spews up from the Chaiten volcano in Chile on May 6, 2008.

Under Pressure

Not all volcanic eruptions are huge explosions. In fact, they are often rather quiet events. And a volcano may have a different kind of eruption each time. How a volcano erupts depends on the pressure that builds inside the magma chamber. High pressure makes magma thick and gooey. Lower pressure in the magma chamber produces thin, runny magma that flows more easily. The greater the pressure, the more explosive the eruption.

When the magma is thin and runny, gas can escape easily. So instead of exploding during an eruption, lava flows gently down

A car is submerged in ash as a result of the 1980 Mount St. Helens eruption in Washington State.

Are Geysers the Same as Volcanoes?

No, geysers are not volcanoes. What erupts from a geyser is boiling-hot water and steam, not lava and ash. However, geysers are usually found near active volcanoes. The water in underground springs close to a volcano's magma chamber heats up. Pressure rises inside it until a spray of hot water squirts out through a crack in the ground. That lowers the pressure in the hot spring, and the geyser stops erupting until the water pressure builds up again. The most famous geyser is Wyoming's Old Faithful, in Yellowstone National Park. It erupts fairly regularly, every 91 minutes on the average. The geyser sends 14,000 to 32,000 liters (3,700 to 8,400 gallons) of water more than 30 meters (100 feet) into the air.

the sides of the volcano. This is the least dangerous type of eruption. People usually have time to run to safety. The volcanoes on the Hawaiian Islands generally have these mild eruptions.

When magma is really thick and sticky, like tar, it traps gas bubbles. The gas keeps building up inside the volcano until finally it explodes. The powerful eruption throws hot molten (melted) rock everywhere, and thick lava oozes out.

The most dangerous, explosive type of volcanic eruption happens when the magma is so thick and sticky that it acts like glue. As the magma at the top cools down, it becomes solid rock, plugging up the crater like a cork in a bottle. Over time—perhaps

Molten lava from the Kilauea volcano streams into the ocean in November 2005. On November 28, about 40 acres of solid lava that had formed at the water's edge collapsed into the sea.

What Is Lava?

Lava is actually magma that has reached Earth's surface. It comes out as hot molten rock and burns up everything it touches—trees, houses, buildings, and people. The lava begins to cool as it flows down the sides of the volcano. Eventually it hardens and becomes solid rock.

hundreds of years—the pressure underneath this plug keeps building. Eventually the volcano bursts in a huge explosion! That's what happened when Mount St. Helens erupted in May 1980.

What Are the Dangers?

Disaster movies often show people dying in a pool of lava. But, lava generally moves so slowly that deaths by lava flows are not very common. So what makes an eruption so deadly? Erupting volcanoes can kill people and destroy property in various ways.

Mauna Loa is the largest volcano on Earth, rising to more than 4 kilometers (2.5 miles) above sea level. The enormous volcano covers half the island of Hawaii.

An explosive eruption sends gases, lava, and hot pieces of rock into the air with tremendous force. The gases that spew out of a volcano are mostly water vapor and carbon dioxide. But there are also small amounts of poisonous gases. These include sulfur compounds, which are very stinky. (Some of them smell like rotten eggs.) These gases can kill people.

The broken-up rocks and other bits of volcanic matter are called pyroclastic material. This material can come in all sorts of shapes and sizes:

- Lapilli are tiny pieces of rock.
- Lava bombs are soft lumps. Most are somewhat rounded, about the size of a tennis ball.
- Volcanic blocks are solid chunks of rock. They can be as big as a car or a house. They can fall miles from the volcano and cause a lot of damage.

Pyroclastic material also includes volcanic ash. It is hard and scratchy, not like the soft ash from a wood fire. The volcanic ash forms a huge cloud that may stretch for miles above the crater. As the ash falls to the ground, it can cover a whole area like a blanket of snow. It is dangerous for people because it can make it difficult to breathe.

Eruptions can also cause gases, hot ash, and pieces of rock to race down the sides of the volcano. These pyroclastic flows can travel as fast as 161 to 241 kilometers (100 to 150 miles) per hour.

Explosive eruptions can also loosen the soil and rocks at the surface, along with snow and ice. These materials may break free and go crashing down the mountain in landslides. When volcanic materials mix with the water in streams flowing down the sides of the mountain, they turn into mud. The mixture rushes down the streams as mudflows, or lahars.

Anak Krakatau (whose name means "Child of Krakatau") rises at the center of an older volcano, Krakatau. The larger volcano erupted violently in 1883, destroying most of the island. Anak Krakatau first appeared in 1930 and is shown here in a 2004 photo. Tectonic forces are now pushing it upward at an alarming rate.

As they start down the mountain, these mudflows are very powerful, ripping out trees and carrying away entire houses in their path. Sometimes lahars contain so much rocky material that they look like fast-moving rivers of wet concrete. Downstream, they bury everything in mud.

As the lava, ash, and rocks spill over the sides of the mountain, they harden into solid rock. Each eruption adds material to the mountain, and it gradually gets taller. Very violent eruptions, however, can blast away the rock and tear down part of the mountain. For example, the big eruption of Mount St. Helens in 1980 blasted a huge crater out of the top of the mountain. Afterward, a series of mild eruptions helped to build a dome inside the crater. Twice the dome was destroyed by powerful eruptions, then built up again. But the peak of Mount St. Helens is still much lower than it was before the 1980 eruption.

The Year Without a Summer

The eruption of Mount Tambora in Indonesia in 1815 affected the whole world, not just the local area. Clouds of dust and gases covered Earth for years, partly blocking out the sunlight and changing the weather. In 1816 it snowed during the summer months in many parts of the United States and Europe. That frigid time was known as "the year without a summer."

Types of Volcanoes

Not all volcanoes are dome-shaped. Actually, there are several main types of volcanoes. They include:

Cinder cone volcano. This is the most common type of volcano. It is formed by loose pieces of lava that fall as cinders or ash close to a single vent. The lava cinders pile up around the vent, producing a steep-sided cone shape. There is usually a crater at the top.

One example is Parícutin, in Mexico. This volcano first appeared in 1943 and built up a 424-meter (1,391 feet) cone in just nine years.

An aerial photograph of Parícutin, a cinder cone volcano in Mexico.

Shield volcano. This kind of volcano is wide, with gently sloping sides. It looks like an ancient warrior's shield. It is formed by a series of slow-moving lava flows. The Hawaiian Islands are made of a long chain of shield volcanoes. One of them is Mauna Loa, the world's largest active volcano.

Composite volcano. Also called a stratovolcano, this is a large, steep-sided volcano that is formed by a series of

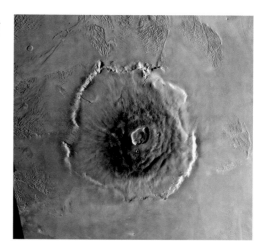

Olympus Mons, on Mars, is a typical shield volcano with a broad top and gently sloping sides.

eruptions. Lava flows over buildups of cinders and ash. Then the new layers of lava are covered by more cinders and ash. Lava may also ooze out through cracks in the sides of the mountain. Composite volcanoes are often the most deadly. Examples are

Mount St. Helens in Washington State, Krakatau in Indonesia, and Mount Pinatubo in the Philippines.

Lava dome volcano. This kind of volcano is formed when very slow-flowing lava piles up around the vent. The dome grows as the pool of magma inside expands. The outer surface cools and breaks apart, spilling volcanic matter down the sides. Lava domes often form in the craters or on the sides of large composite volcanoes. Examples are Mount Pelée in the Caribbean island of Martinique and the lava dome that has formed inside the crater of Mount St. Helens.

This 1989 photo of Mount St. Helens shows a small lava dome forming in the crater of the large composite volcano.

Crater Lake in Oregon, shown in a 1987 photo, is a typical caldera volcano.

Caldera volcano. This volcano is formed when a huge eruption destroys the top of the volcano, leaving a huge crater that may later fill with water. Crater Lake in Oregon is an example of a caldera volcano.

UNDERWATER VOLCANOES

The most well-known volcanoes

are on land. But actually, most of the volcanoes on Earth are hidden underwater. Scientists call these underwater volcanoes submarine volcanoes. Several thousand active submarine volcanoes have been discovered. But some scientists believe there may be as many as a million on the ocean floor.[1] That's more than 660 times the number of volcanoes on dry land!

Are Underwater Volcanoes Different?

Most underwater volcanoes are found near the edges of tectonic plates along the ocean floor. These areas are called mid-ocean ridges. As the plates move apart, magma comes

Diver Bud Turpin observes as pillow lava erupts underwater from Kilauea Volcano in Hawaii.

up through the cracks. But underwater volcanoes erupt different-ly than those on land.

Some volcanoes form in shallow water. When they erupt, they may blast steam and bits of rocks high above the ocean surface. The steam is formed when seawater flows into the volcano's vents. The hot magma superheats the water. When lava erupts from a shallow submarine volcano, the surrounding water may cool the

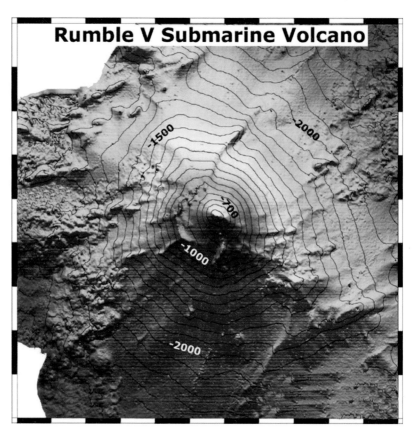

An aerial-view map of the Rumble V submarine volcano. The numbers on the map indicate depth below the surface in meters.

lava so quickly that it breaks up into tiny pieces. The "black sand" beaches of Hawaii were formed in this way.

Most submarine volcanoes are located in deep ocean waters. These volcanoes are under tremendous pressure from the surrounding ocean. The high pressure prevents gases from escaping. Lava oozes out and forms solid "pillows." The pillow lava piles up around the vent, forming a steep-sided cone. As a deepwater volcano grows larger and its peak gets closer to the ocean surface, it may start to erupt violently. Cinders, ash, and other pyroclastic matter blasts out of the vent and adds to the cone.

Eventually, submarine volcanoes may build up high

How Does Pressure Work in Submarine Volcanoes?

Pressure is a pushing force. If you were in a diving suit at the ocean bottom, the weight of all the water above you would be pressing against your suit. (You wouldn't feel this because the air pressure inside your suit pushes outward with the same amount of force.) The deeper you go in the ocean, the more water there is above you. So the pressure is greater. That is why shallow-water volcanoes can blast out eruptions into the air above the surface. The pressure of magma inside them is greater than the pressure of the water above them. But in deepwater volcanoes, the water pressure is so great that the magma just oozes out.

On November 14, 1963, on the southwest coast of Iceland, fishermen watched an amazing sight: a volcanic eruption blasting out of the water. The eruption began about 130 meters (425 feet) beneath the ocean surface. It continued for the next three and a half years. During that time, the lava flowing out of the volcano gradually built an island with an area of 3 square kilometers (1 square mile). The peak rose more than 171 meters (560 feet) above sea level. This new island was named Surtsey, after Surtur, a fire giant from Icelandic legend.

Only scientists are allowed to visit the island of Surtsey. Since its birth, researchers have watched the island grow and develop. In 1965, plants were the first signs of life on Surtsey. Now much of the island is covered by plants—at least 60 different kinds have been found. Many other living things have made Surtsey their home, including a variety of insects and birds. Sea animals, such as seals, sea stars, and sea urchins, also live near the island.[2]

enough to rise above the ocean surface. That is how islands like those that make up Hawaii are formed. This process can take thousands of years, but explosive eruptions may help to build islands much faster.

When an underwater volcano erupts, the explosion may cause enormous ocean waves. These waves, called tsunamis, speed through the water and build up to tremendous heights—

Volcanic activity left black sand on the beach in Maui, Hawaii.

up to 30 meters (100 feet) or more! The Kick-'em-Jenny under-water volcano in the Caribbean, for example, has erupted ten times since 1939. Twice the eruptions produced minor tsunamis that flooded roads in nearby Barbados.[3]

Most tsunamis, however, are caused by underwater earthquakes or eruptions of volcanoes on islands. One tsunami occurred in 1883, when Krakatau, a volcano in Indonesia, exploded. The volcano was on an island, then called Krakatau. The blast destroyed more than two-thirds of the island. Within an hour or two, the tsunami, with waves up to 37 meters (120 feet) high, flooded 295 towns and villages in the area.[4]

Living on the Edge

Most ocean plants and animals live near the ocean's surface, where they depend on the sun's energy for survival. Sunlight cannot reach deep ocean waters, so temperatures are usually too cold—about 2 degrees Celsius (36 degrees Fahrenheit)—to support life. But scientists have discovered that a whole community of life

Black smoke emerges from a mid-ocean ridge hydrothermal vent.

survives very well around gaps in the ocean floor called hydrothermal vents. These underwater hot springs are often found near submarine volcanoes.

When a hydrothermal vent erupts, it spews superheated water—as hot as 400 degrees Celsius (752 degrees Fahrenheit)—that kills every living thing nearby. Soon, as the area cools to below 100 degrees Celsius (212 degrees Fahrenheit), new life appears around the vents.

Heat is a form of energy. Bacteria living in the deep sea can use this energy and sulfur compounds in the water to make food.

They gather around the vents and multiply. The bacteria, in turn, become food for sea animals such as crabs, tube worms, and mussels, which also gather around the vents. In just one year, the number of species living around a vent can double.

Although some animals can thrive around hydrothermal vents, volcanoes on land can be very dangerous to humans. How can people protect themselves from these unpredictable forces of nature?

Pillow lava (above) is a rock formation consisting of rounded masses of solidified lava. It forms when molten rock (lava) issues from an underwater volcanic vent.

STAYING SAFE

Most of the time, volcanoes give clues

before they are going to erupt. Before its big eruption in 1980, Mount St. Helens gave plenty of warning signs that it was "waking up." For many weeks, scientists kept a close watch on the volcano's activity. They did not know exactly when Mount St. Helens was going to erupt, but they knew it would be soon. They warned the U.S. Forest Service, which then evacuated people living in areas that were dangerously close to the volcano. Though fifty-seven people died in the eruption, the early warning probably saved thousands of lives.

A Javanese man walks in the shadow of Mount Merapi as it spews volcanic smoke in Babadan village, Central Java, Indonesia, on April 22, 2006.

Buried Alive

When Mount Vesuvius began to erupt in A.D. 79, panic spread through the city of Pompeii, in southern Italy. Rocks and ash rained down on the city, piling up at a rate of 15 centimeters (6 inches) per hour. Then, suddenly, a choking cloud of hot gases, ash, and rock poured out of the mountain at tremendous speeds. No one in its path could escape.

When the eruption ended, nineteen hours after it began, the entire city of Pompeii was buried under a layer of ash 8 meters (26 feet) deep. Heavy rains then turned the ash solid like concrete. Nearly seventeen hundred years later, archaeologists dug out the buried city. They found houses, furniture, statues, and jewelry. Hollows in the volcanic rock formed the outlines of two thousand of the volcano's victims. Even the expressions on their faces were preserved.

This figure of a girl trapped in a pottery shop in Pompeii when Vesuvius erupted was cast using a hollow in the solid ash as a mold.

Predicting an Eruption

Generally, volcanologists cannot predict *exactly* when a volcano will erupt. A volcano can show signs of activity for days, months, or even years before it finally erupts. Sometimes, a period of rumbling does not lead to an eruption after all. However, predicting a volcanic eruption is important so that people can have time to leave for a safer place. Fortunately, volcanologists have a number of ways to help predict future eruptions.

A volcanologist explores near Mauna Loa Volcano, where the lava can run as hot as 1,145 degrees Celsius (2,093 degrees Fahrenheit).

Why Do People Live Near Volcanoes?

Volcanoes can be dangerous. But living and working near them can also have some benefits. For many people, volcanoes are:

- A great place to grow crops. Lava and ash are rich in minerals from deep inside Earth. After an eruption, these minerals become part of the soil. For example, the island of Java, in Indonesia, is one of the world's top rice-growing areas. Farms there are located around volcanoes.

- A great place for mining precious minerals and gemstones. These valuable products—such as gold, copper, silver, lead, zinc, and diamonds—have been created within the magma deep inside Earth for thousands or millions of years. Volcanic eruptions carry them to the surface.

- A good source of geothermal energy. Geothermal energy is heat energy that comes from inside Earth. This energy source can be used to produce electricity. More than twenty countries around the world—including the United States, Italy, New Zealand, and Iceland—use geothermal energy.

One way is by studying the rock and ash formed by past eruptions. Volcanic eruptions sometimes occur in a pattern. So studying a volcano's past eruptions may give clues to possible future eruptions.

Meanwhile, volcanologists use special equipment that checks a volcano's activity day and night. Earthquakes are probably the best clues that a volcano is becoming more active. These earthquakes are caused by magma rising to the surface and moving rocks around. Seismometers are instruments that measure the earthquakes' vibrations around the volcano.

Instruments also measure the temperature inside the volcano and the amount of gases seeping out of it. Another clue is a bulge or a crack in the side of the volcano. An instrument called a tiltmeter measures a tilt, or angle, in the rock as a bulge begins to form. Other devices test for mudflows and the temperature of nearby streams and rivers.

Volcanologists also depend on satellites to detect volcanic activity on Earth. A satellite is a spacecraft that circles the planet. It can collect information about anyplace in the world. The satellite then sends the information back to a control center on Earth. For example, a satellite in space can measure the temperature inside a volcano on Earth. The readings are sent to a computer, which turns them into images.

In Case of Emergency

If you live near a volcano, there are some things you and your family can do to help you stay safe. There are probably special volcano shelters in your area. Know where they are and the fastest way to get to them. It is important to have an emergency plan.

Scientists install a tiltmeter on Mount St. Helens.

Your school may have regular volcano drills to practice what to do. Pay attention so you will remember if a real eruption occurs.

At home, keep a kit with emergency supplies handy. It should include:

- Flashlight and batteries
- Battery-operated radio
- First aid kit
- Emergency food and water
- Dust masks, goggles, and hard hats

A watertube tilt pot (above) is a special tilt measurement instrument used by scientists studying volcanoes.

Listen for volcano warnings on the radio or look for information on the Internet or TV, and follow the instructions. If the local officials say your area should be evacuated, do not waste time. Leave as quickly as you can.

If a nearby volcano is erupting, wear goggles to protect your eyes. Use a dust mask or damp cloth over your face to keep from breathing volcanic ash. Wear long sleeves and long pants to help protect your skin. Watch out for fast-moving mudflows, which usually follow the path of rivers or streams.

Meanwhile, local emergency workers will be doing all they can to help. For example, they may use explosives to dig trenches to guide lava flows away from farms and villages.

Volcanoes are tremendous forces of nature. We can't stop them from erupting. But most volcanoes do not erupt very often. And they usually give warning signs before they erupt. So even people who live or vacation in areas with volcanoes will have enough time to find safety.

Children wear hard hats to protect them from debris falling from the Sakurajima Volcano in Japan. Sakurajima is an active stratovolcano located very close to Kagoshima City, where more than 540,000 people live.

CHAPTER NOTES

CHAPTER 1 A SLEEPING GIANT AWAKENS

1. Steven R. Brantley and Bobbie Myers, "Mount St. Helens—From the 1980 Eruption to 2000," *USGS Fact Sheet*, March 2000, <http://pubs.usgs .gov/fs/2000/fs036-00/fs036-00.pdf> (May 22, 2007).

2. Ibid.

3. Ibid.

4. Ibid.

5. Ibid.

6. Lyn Topinka, "Mount St. Helens Returns to Slumber," *USGS/ Cascades Volcano Observatory, Vancouver, Washington,* July 10, 2008, <http://vulcan.wr.usgs.gov/Volcanoes/MSH/Eruption04/Monitoring/ July2008/> (August 14, 2008).

CHAPTER 2 UNDERSTANDING VOLCANOES

1. "Volcanoes and People: Volcanoes! Lesson 6," *U.S. Geological Survey,* 1997, < http://erg.usgs.gov/isb/pubs/teachers-packets/volcanoes/lesson6/ lesson6.html> (August 20, 2008).

2. Cheryl Ernst, "Life in Mars?" *Mālamalama,* January 2005, <http:// www.hawaii.edu/malamalama/archive/downloads/0501_all.pdf> (August 14, 2008).

CHAPTER 3 WHEN A VOLCANO ERUPTS

1. "Volcano Scientists Go to School to Learn How to Track Volcanic Ash," *U.S. Geological Survey,* February 22, 2007, <http://hvo.wr.usgs.gov/ volcanowatch/2007/07_02_22.html> (June 4, 2007).

CHAPTER 4 UNDERWATER VOLCANOES

1. "Submarine Eruptions—Volcanoes on the Rise," *U.S. Geological Survey*, July 14, 2005, <http://hvo.wr.usgs.gov/volcanowatch/2005/05_07_14.html> (August 20, 2008).

2. "Surtsey, Iceland's Island of Fire," *Explore North*, n.d., <http://explorenorth.com/library/weekly/aa042601a.htm> (August 15, 2008); "Surtsey," *UNESCO: World Heritage*, July 8, 2008, <http://whc.unesco.org/en/list/1267> (August 15, 2008).

3. Lyn Topinka, "Kick 'Em Jenny Volcano, West Indies," *USGS/Cascades Volcano Observatory, Vancouver, Washington*, December 12, 2001, <http://vulcan.wr.usgs.gov/Volcanoes/WestIndies/KickEmJenny/description_kick_em_jenny.html> (August 15, 2008).

4. George Pararas-Carayannis, "The Great Tsunami of August 26, 1883 from the Explosion of the Krakatau Volcano ("Krakatoa") in Indonesia," excerpts from *Some of the World's Greatest Disasters,*"1997, <http://www.drgeorgepc.com/Tsunami1883Krakatoa.html> (August 15, 2008).

GLOSSARY

active volcano—A volcano that is currently erupting or has recently erupted.

caldera—A large bowl-shaped crater that forms when an empty magma chamber collapses or when the top of a volcano is blown off during a violent eruption.

cinder-cone volcano—A cone-shaped volcano mountain formed by repeated eruptions in which cinders and ash build up close to the vent.

composite volcano—A cone-shaped volcano formed by alternating layers of lava and ash; also known as a stratovolcano.

core—The innermost part of Earth.

crater—A bowl-shaped opening at the top of a volcano. It forms when matter is lost during an eruption.

crust—The outer layer of Earth.

dormant volcano—A volcano that appears inactive but is capable of erupting.

eruption—A sudden, violent outburst; the ejection of molten rock, steam, or other matter from a volcano or geyser.

extinct volcano—A volcano that last erupted a long time ago and is not considered capable of erupting again.

geologist—A scientist who studies the structure and history of Earth.

geothermal energy—Heat energy from inside Earth.

geyser—A hot spring that sends up fountainlike jets of water and steam; usually found near volcanoes.

hot spots—Regions in which magma seeps through weak spots in Earth's crust.

hydrothermal vents—Gaps in the ocean floor where superheated water erupts.

lahar—A combination of volcanic matter and water that flows downward, destroying everything in its path; mudflow.

landslide—The falling or sliding of large amounts of soil and rocks downhill at tremendous speeds.

lapilli—Tiny pieces of rock ejected from an erupting volcano; it means "little stones."

lava—The melted rock that comes out of an erupting volcano, or the rock formed when it becomes solid.

lava bombs—Rocks formed from softened lava that fall close to the vent.

lava dome volcano—A volcano that is formed when slow-flowing lava piles up around the vent.

magma—Hot, melted rock beneath or within Earth's crust.

magma chamber—A giant pool of molten rock (magma) beneath Earth's surface.

mantle—The layer of Earth between the crust and the core.

mid-ocean ridge—A region in which a group of volcanoes forms along the ocean floor.

molten—Melted.

pillow lava—Lava that formed pillow-shaped rocks.

pressure—The pushing force of an object or fluid against something else.

pyroclastic—Formed by volcanic action.

pyroclastic flow—A mixture of lava and hot gases that may flow rapidly down a volcanic mountain after an eruption.

Ring of Fire—A horseshoe-shaped region along the edges of the Pacific Ocean where more than 75 percent of Earth's active volcanoes are found.

seismometer—An instrument that measures the vibrations of earthquakes.

shield volcano—A volcano with the shape of a low, wide dome, formed by repeated flows of lava.

submarine volcano—An underwater volcano.

tectonic plates—The large pieces of rock that make up Earth's crust.

tiltmeter—An instrument that measures changes in the angle of Earth's surface.

tsunami—An unusually large ocean wave produced by an earthquake or undersea volcanic eruption.

vent—The opening in a volcano from which gases, lava, and other volcanic matter escape.

volcanic blocks—Solid chunks of lava that may be very large.

volcano—An opening in Earth's crust through which hot matter escapes from the mantle below; or the cone-shaped mountain formed around such an opening by the buildup of lava and ash.

volcanologist—A scientist who studies volcanoes.

FURTHER READING

BOOKS

Green, Jen. *Understanding Volcanoes and Earthquakes.* New York: Powerkids Press, 2008.

Rubin, Ken. *Volcanoes & Earthquakes.* New York: Simon & Schuster Children's Publishing, 2007.

Rusch, Elizabeth. *Will It Blow?: Become a Volcano Detective at Mount St. Helens.* Seattle, Wash.: Sasquatch Books, 2007.

Sengupta, Monalisa. *Volcanoes and Earthquakes.* New York: Powerkids Press, 2007.

Stewart, Melissa. *Earthquakes and Volcanoes FYI.* New York: HarperCollins, 2008.

INTERNET RESOURCES

"Learn About Volcanoes," Lyn Topinka, U.S. Geological Survey (USGS)
<http://vulcan.wr.usgs.gov/Outreach/AboutVolcanoes/framework.html>
Frequently asked questions about volcanoes, including a list of the deadliest eruptions since 1500, plus links to other volcano Web sites.

"Pompeii: The Last Day," Discovery Kids
<http://kids.discovery.com/games/pompeii/pompeii.html>
Information about volcanoes and how to build a virtual erupting volcano in VolcanoExplorer; the Pompeii story in text, pictures, and videos; and a quiz to see if you would have survived the eruption.

"Volcano World," Oregon Space Grant Consortium
<http://volcano.oregonstate.edu/>
Reports on active volcanoes; volcano legends from around the world; interviews with volcanologists and information on volcanology careers; National Parks with volcanoes; and special fun features "4-Kids," including games and puzzles, virtual field trips, and stories.

INDEX